# BARBECUE COOKBOOK

## MARY BERRY

A MARTIN BOOK

Martin Books
8 Market Passage, Cambridge CB2 3PF

First published 1979
© Smedley-HP Foods Limited and Mary Berry 1979
ISBN 0 85941 089 7

*Conditions of sale*
All rights reserved. No part of this publication may be reproduced, stored in a retrieval system or transmitted, in any form or by any means, electronic, mechanical, photocopying, recording or otherwise, without the prior permission of the copyright owners.

The photographs on the following pages are reproduced by kind permission of:
*Danepak Ltd*, page 88
*M.E.A.T.*, page 41
*National Magazine Co Ltd*, pages 9 and 17
*New Zealand Lamb Information Bureau*, page 44
*Syndication International Ltd*, pages 13 and 76.

Acknowledgement is also due to *Frank Odell Ltd* for the back cover photograph and for the loan of various items of barbecue equipment to Mary Berry for trying out recipes.

The front cover photograph shows a twin portable hibachi barbecue; sardines with devilled butter; beefburgers cordon bleu; and chicken parcels.

Cover design and text layout by Ken Vail

Typesetting by BEST Limited

Printed and bound in Great Britain by Hazell Watson & Viney Limited, Aylesbury, Bucks

# Foreword

*by* Julian Lea, *Marketing, Sales and Distribution Director, Lea & Perrins Limited*

Barbecuing provides the perfect opportunity for a party. It is the new fun way to entertain friends – on the spur of the moment or as a more sophisticated, planned event. It livens up weekends and holiday times for all the family with a tasty change from conventional meals. Nor does barbecuing have to be a summer-only activity – many people are now barbecuing all the year round.

For the beginner there is a daunting array of barbecues and barbecue equipment on the market, which makes selection difficult. There is also the problem of finding suitable recipes and choosing the right foods for the occasion.

To help solve these problems and set you on the road to successful barbecuing, Lea & Perrins Limited are delighted to sponsor this informative book by cookery expert Mary Berry. As the makers of the original and genuine Worcestershire Sauce, which is an indispensable ingredient in the making of barbecue sauces, bastes and marinades, we are sure that you will enjoy the imaginative recipes which Mary has created and tested or collected from fellow barbecue enthusiasts. Her down-to-earth advice on the art of successful barbecuing is invaluable.

Have fun and happy barbecuing!

*Julian Lea.*

# Acknowledgements

A big thank you for all the ideas, recipes and hints I've been given by keen barbecuing friends, especially to Roz for her smashing Bennett Sauce and many tips, and to Deke for his encouragement and Sardines with sea salt. The Barbecued Baked Beans come from the Henchers, avid barbecuers in all weathers!

I should also thank Paul, my husband, for being chief stoker and fire manager and the children, who would have breakfast on the barbecue given the chance!

My special thanks, too, to Clare Blunt for her meticulous trying out and development of recipes. They have been tested on several barbecues, some simple and some more luxurious.

*Mary Berry*

*Note:* Quantities of ingredients are given in both metric (g, ml) and imperial (oz, pt) measures; you can use either, *but not a mixture of both*, in any given recipe.

# Contents

*Foreword* 3

*Acknowledgements* 4

**Introducing Barbecues**
*What Barbecuing is all About* 8
*How to Build Your Own Barbecue* 10
Improvised grills 10
Permanent structures 11
Movable wheelbarrow barbecue 14
*Barbecues to Buy* 15
Hibachis 15
Party barbecues 16
Picnic barbecue 16
Covered grills 16
Wagon grill 18
Gas-fired barbecues 18
Smoke'n Pit 19
*Fuel for the Barbecue* 20
Wood charcoal pieces 20
Charcoal briquettes 20
Wood 20
Gas 21
*Lighting the Fire* 21
Firelighters 21
Time taken in lighting 22
Ready to cook 23
Keeping the fire going 23
Aromatic fires 23
Varying the heat 23
Putting the fire out 23
*Cleaning and Caring for the Barbecue* 24
Methods of cleaning 24
Storage 25
*Safety First* 25
Rules for safety 25
Children 26
*Barbecue Extras* 26
*Planning a Party* 31
Setting the scene 31
The menu 31
Cooking and serving 32
Getting rid of rubbish 32
*How to Buy and Cook the Basic Meat and Poultry* 33
Buying hints 33
Cooking times for each side 33

**Variety Recipes**
Barbecued Chicken Drumsticks 36
Devilled Chicken Joints 37
Chicken Lyonnaise 38
Barbecued Chicken Parcels 39
Marinated Indian Chicken 40
Lamburgers 40
Lamb Chops Ratatouille 42
Lamb Noisettes 43
Greek Meatballs 45
American Beefburgers 45
Beefburgers Cordon Bleu 46
Pork Sausages 46
Frankfurter Rolls 47
Gammon with Honey and Orange 48
Savoury Bacon Rolls 48
Brochettes of Liver 49

5

Bacon, Kidney and
  Sausage Kebabs  50
Chicken Liver Kebabs  51
Chinese Pork Kebabs  51
Pork Fruity Kebabs  52
Pork and Pineapple
  Kebabs  53
Lamb Kebabs  54
Fishermen's Kebabs  55
Salmon Fishcakes  56
Fresh Sardines  56
Trout with Horseradish
  Butter  57
Devilled Mackerel  57
Savoury Sausage Risotto  58

**Bastes and Sauces, etc.**
*Bastes*
Spicy Tomato Baste  60
Chinese Basting Sauce  60
'No Cook' Barbecue Baste  61
*Sauces*
Tomato Bennett Sauce  61
Tomato Sauce  62
Barbecue Sauce  63
Piquant Sauce  64
*Dips*
Cranberry Dip  65
Savoury Topping  65
Sweetcorn and Bacon
  Topping  66
Pineapple and Cheese
  Topping  66
Easy Curry Mayonnaise  67
Mustard Mayonnaise  67
Tomato Dip  68
Soured Cream Topping
  for Potatoes  68
*Marinades*
Fresh Herb Marinade  69
Red Wine Marinade  69
*Savoury Butters*
Devilled Butter  70

Horseradish Butter  70
Curry Butter  71
Maître d'Hôtel Butter  71
Garlic Butter  71
Garlic Bread  72

**Good Things to go
with Barbecues**
*Soups*
Gaspacho  74
Chilled Lettuce and
  Cucumber Soup  75
Onion Soup  76
Cornish Crab Soup  77
Fried Bread Kebabs  77
*Salads and Vegetables*
Tomato and Onion Salad  78
French Dressing  78
French Dressed
  Mushrooms  79
Cucumber and Dill Salad  79
Green Salad  80
Salad Niçoise  81
Yogurt, Mint and
  Cucumber Salad  82
Piquant Cheese and
  Carrots  82
Potato Burgers  83
Barbecued Baked Beans  84
Pilaff  86
Indian Rice  87
Corn on the Cob  87
Jacket Potatoes  88
*Sweets*
Fresh Melon Sorbet  89
Coffee Meringue Gâteau  90
Fresh Fruit Salad  91
Austrian Rum Torte  92
Caramelised Bananas  93
Raspberry Shortbread  94
*Drinks*
Cider and Orange Cooler  95
Fresh Lemon and Lime  95

# Introducing Barbecues

# WHAT BARBECUING IS ALL ABOUT

Barbecue! How lovely it sounds, conjuring up pictures of open-air meals, delicious steaks, warm summer evenings and wood smoke! The reality may be different. Apart from the open-air touch, the steaks have become beefburgers, the warm evening a time of dodging drops of rain or smearing bare arms with anti-midge cream, and the wood smoke relatively non-existent if the grill fire is working efficiently. But somehow the magic remains. I have never met anyone who can claim in all honesty not to feel the smallest thrill at the thought of a barbecue.

As with so many things to do with the great outdoors, the Americans have turned the barbecue into a fine art, and Britain is now rapidly following suit. A century ago in America, the barbecue meant a vast alfresco feast – probably one in which the entire community joined – where a whole ox or hog (or several if it were a large community!) would be slowly roasted over an open fire. There would be music and dancing and a great deal of merrymaking.

The word itself has at least two origins, according to the experts. Some say it comes from Haiti, where a *barbacoa* means a framework used for cooking or drying meat over a fire. Others prefer a corruption of *"de barbe en queue"* (from beard to tail), which was how French settlers in Louisiana described a method of roasting a goat. Either way, the word is firmly established in the English language, its meaning instantly recognisable and immediately mouth-watering.

In essence, to barbecue is to cook meat over a grill which is usually fired by charcoal. In practice, since charcoal as it burns gives off carbon monoxide, the cooking has to be carried on out of doors, unless the indoor fireplace is really well ventilated. And as outdoor cooking is more fun with lots of people around, a barbecue often indicates a party.

All sorts of barbecuing equipment are available, the grills themselves ranging from very elaborate pieces with rotary spits mechanically operated, controllable air vents, covers and wind shields, to simple pack-away models for taking on picnics. Alternatively, you can build a barbecue yourself.

Many people start with the basic grid-and-pan types for the very laudable reason that they tend to be the cheapest. This is a wise policy if you are a complete newcomer to the pleasure of barbecues. I say pleasure because that is how I view a barbecue, and my family are hooked as well, but yours may not be and there is no point in laying out a lot of money unless it is really going to be worth while.

A super spread for a bonfire night party.

Others start by building a very simple brick barbecue in the garden or improvising one from an old biscuit or roasting tin. The advantage of the latter is that it does allow you to test your enjoyment of barbecues without costing you anything more than the price of a bag of charcoal and a packet of firelighters. If you then find that you and the family are really much happier sitting down at a proper dining table to a meal cooked on the stove in your kitchen, well, no harm has been done, no household budget gravely exceeded and you've learned something about yourselves anyway.

## HOW TO BUILD YOUR OWN BARBECUE

**Improvised grills.** The biscuit or roasting tin barbecue mentioned above is probably the easiest to improvise in a back garden simply because the materials required are the most readily available. Most people have an old biscuit tin. Remove the lid first, then punch holes in the sides of the tin near the base. Stand the tin in a suitable spot on the patio or in the garden and place the rack from a grill-pan or a piece of

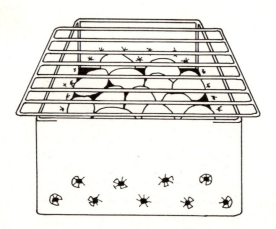

chicken wire (preferably double-thickness but single-thickness will do) on top. Hey presto, there's your barbecue, awaiting only a layer of glowing coals at the bottom of the tin for the outdoor supper to start.

Another improvisation is to use a large flowerpot as the container for the charcoal, raising the pot on bricks in order to get enough draught for the fire. If you have no suitable grill-pan rack and the chicken wire is being used to keep the chickens from straying, an oven grid or old refrigerator rack (not a plastic one of course) will do as well. Loose bricks built up to form a support for the rack are also barbecue material but remember to leave a few gaps in the bricks to form air holes.

**Permanent structures.** The sole disadvantage of a permanent barbecue is its immobility. You are stuck with it in the position you first chose for it. So before getting to work with bricks and mortar, try the site out with a portable barbecue first. Make the test on several occasions so that you know how it will behave under different wind conditions. The barbecue should be out of the prevailing wind but not in too sheltered a position where there might not be enough draught to get the fire going properly. Test, too, for smoke. If the site you choose fills the barbecue area with smoke, all enjoyment will be severely handicapped. It should also be readily accessible from the house, ideally near to the back door, so that trips to fetch food, or plates, or anything you have forgotten, do not become expeditions each time.

Once you have settled on the site it is wise to keep the design fairly simple. A corner of a patio wall often makes a good position, providing a natural back for the grill. Furthermore, the presence of a low wall nearby provides extra seating for guests at parties.

If you are good at do-it-yourself, it helps to incorporate a charcoal store into the design. Normally, this takes the form of a brick-built cupboard with hinged door at the front. A concrete paving slab makes an effective roof to the cupboard and adds a useful working surface as well. For the grilling area, the side of the cupboard doubles as one side of the fire section. The other is simply a double-thickness brick wall built to match the height of the cupboard. A low brick step, two courses high, should enclose the front. Specially hardened fire bricks are the best material for the inside of the barbecue, but, if you feel that these are too expensive, it may be possible to buy broken fire bricks cheaply from your local builders merchant.

As you build the walls up, incorporate flat pieces of metal between the courses at the appropriate height so that the edges project to form runners on which the fire pan and grid can rest. An old roasting tin makes an effective fire pan. The width of the barbecue depends on the size of the pan. At the same time, metal supports for a spit can be cemented into place. These need be no more than L-shaped brackets fitted with the short arm of the L in the brickwork and the long arm projecting above the top of the barbecue. Notches in the top take a simple crank-handle shaped spit.

For safety's sake, pave the area immediately surrounding the barbecue. Paving stones are best, bedded on to a layer of builders sand over well-rammed hardcore. They are easy to brush clean too. If the lawn grows right up to the edge of the barbecue, not only is it difficult to cut properly, but it may also become slippery and worn if you use your barbecue a lot.

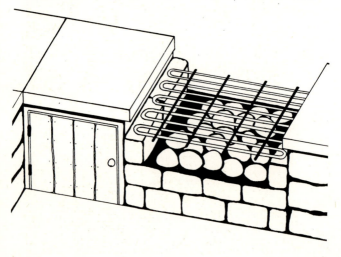

A home-built barbecue, set on the gravel drive for safety.

**Movable wheelbarrow barbecue.** Great friends of mine have hit on a most effective way of making themselves a mobile barbecue. They simply use an old metal wheelbarrow! First of all, they line the wheelbarrow with a double layer of foil. Then they place twin lines of bricks on top. The charcoal goes in the hollow between the bricks and the food on an old oven grid shelf, which rests on the bricks. Part of the grid each side overlaps the bricks, which gives an area for keeping food hot and warming space for bread.

The great joy of this ingenious example of do-it-yourself is that the barbecue can be moved wherever it is wanted. In windy weather it is usually possible to find a sheltered spot somewhere in the garden, or if it is raining the barbecue could stand in a barn or garage. Remember, for safety's sake, to leave the barn or garage doors open. Again for safety reasons, try to select a suitable site before you light the fire and avoid moving the wheelbarrow while the coals are hot.

# BARBECUES TO BUY

You may decide, like hundreds of other people, that do-it-yourself is not for you. In this case, your main problem is choosing the barbecue most suitable for you. There is a large range of manufactured barbecues on the market and you would be wise to look at as many as possible and study the brochures before laying out what could be a large sum of money.

One way of making up your mind is to study the barbecues belonging to your friends and acquaintances. Try to see them in operation, if possible, or at least ask about the advantages and disadvantages. Some people start with small ones, progressing to something bigger later on. Even then the original barbecue can still come in useful – as interest in barbecues grows, so the menus become more elaborate and small grills make handy supplements to the main one.

It can, however, help you to know what barbecues are available. I have tried to list as many types as possible and to point out their virtues as well as their faults and the reasons for both. After all, one barbecue fanatic's fault is another's virtue and only you know exactly what you require.

**Hibachis.** These are perhaps the simplest form of barbecue and also one of the cheapest to buy. *Hibachi* is a Japanese word meaning small heater and, applied to a barbecue, it describes a solid cast-iron fire box fitted with a grill. It can be circular or rectangular and some models are sold with a fold-away stand or detachable legs with wheels. The charcoal fire rests in the bottom of the fire box, which should be at least 3 in. (7 cm) deep. There are draught controls in the side to help with lighting the fire and control the cooking heat. The main disadvantage of the hibachi is that the centre of the grill tends to get hotter than the perimeter, so that, although in theory there should be room to cook for six people, it is better for four. It is, however, possible to buy double-grill or triple-grill hibachis, which of course increases the number you can cook for. Nevertheless, because they are small, they are readily portable and may be placed in any suitable spot in the garden or patio. The latest is the twin portable hibachi with two 12 in. (30 cm) diameter bowls. If it is a barbecue for, say, two or three, light just one side of the barbecue. This is a very neat, practical and sturdy barbecue which folds compactly.

**Party barbecues.** The simplest of these is very like the hibachi in principle, except that the fire box is a shallow tray and it is usually mounted on legs. It is often known as a 'brazier barbecue' and the grill may be revolved so that you do not have to lean over the heat of the fire in order to reach the food. Sometimes it is possible to adjust the height of the grill.

A large brazier with, say 24 in. (60 cm) diameter grill should be able to cope with food for around 20 people. It is an advantage to have one with a windshield to shelter the barbecue in windy weather.

**Picnic barbecue.** A smaller version of the brazier, this is made to pack away so that it can be stowed in the boot of the car or strapped to a rucksack. Most picnic barbecues have 12 in. (30 cm) diameter grills, which gives sufficient cooking area for about four people. These are usually lightweight, about 2 lb (0.9 kg), and are inexpensive to buy.

**Covered grills.** The advantage of the cover is that it turns the grill into a kind of outdoor oven, which means that you can regulate the cooking time more precisely and no basting is necessary. Vents in the base may be opened or closed according to the amount of draught required to get the fire going and thereafter used to control the heat. The dome, which can be

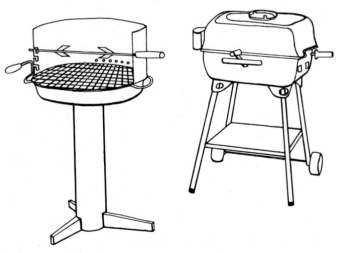

Double hibachi and some long-handled utensils.

used as a hood when it is open, also has a controllable vent. All these help to make fuel consumption very economic and some have a battery-operated spit. At the end of the evening, putting out the fire is not a matter of quenching or dousing: you simply close the vents, thus cutting off the oxygen supply and the fire is dead in about 20 minutes. The inside of the covered grill is left clean and charcoal briquettes dry so that they can easily be used again.

**Wagon grill.** This is a wheeled trolley, surmounted by a covered barbecue and is fitted with many of the extras usually found on modern ovens. It is perfect for those who are attracted by the idea of an outdoor barbecue party, but are not prepared to put up with the guesswork. The extras include such things as gauges for measuring the oven temperature, heat-resistant glass panels in the door so that you can see the food cooking without disturbing it, warming ovens for keeping food and plates hot, and storage cabinets for those who like to have a place for everything. The distance between the food grill and the fire pan can be adjusted and most models are fitted with motorised spits. The shape of this type of barbecue is normally rectangular but some are cylindrical and, although it has wheels and is therefore mobile, it does tend to be somewhat cumbersome. It can be wheeled into a garage or outhouse for storage in the winter.

**Gas-fired barbecues.** The differences between these and other barbecues lies in the fuel. Otherwise they are very similar to the braziers in appearance, although some are fitted with covers. The heat for cooking comes from lumps of lava rock or artificial rock, which do not burn but are heated up by the presence of a gas-burner. The temperature can be controlled by a knob. They have their own cylinder of bottled gas which clips on to the base of the unit. The advantage of these barbecues, apart from the ease of firing, is that they do not give off dangerous fumes and can therefore be used under a canopy for shelter and usually they have two controls 'high' and 'low'. I have been testing a gas barbecue all summer and am thrilled with the results. I cook most foods on low, slowly browning kebabs, chicken joints and sausages. The great plus of a gas barbecue is that the heat is almost instant and you can barbecue just when you want and where you want, as they

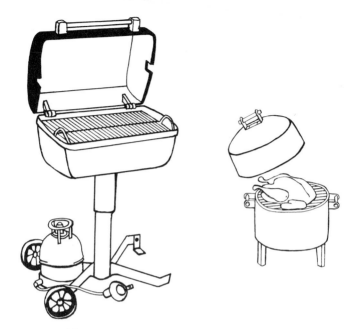

are portable on wheels. The temperature is even and controllable. Most have spits run off batteries if you want them.

**Smoke'n Pit.** Cooking on any barbecue grill is often a slow business, which may or may not be intentional. Smoke'n pit, a new development in outdoor cooking from America, makes a virtue of long, slow cooking. In appearance, it is rather like a boiler or tea urn, and is made of steel, with a baked-on enamel finish. Inside, however, it is a three-tier affair – fire pan at the bottom, water pan in the middle and grid for the food on top. The introduction of the water pan makes this type of barbecue unique and its aim is to keep the temperature slow and even to retain the natural moistness of the food. Aromatic wood chips and chunks are usually added to the fire, which gives a truly appetising flavour to the food, but increases the cooking time; without the wood chips, cooking is faster. Juices and fat dripping from the food fall into the water pan and the liquid can afterwards be used as a base for gravy or sauce. Without the cover and water pan and by moving the fire pan closer to the food, the Smoke'n pit becomes an ordinary barbecue grill. To increase the capacity of the cooker an additional section, complete with grid, can be placed between the base and the cover.

## FUEL FOR THE BARBECUE

Most people use charcoal for the simple reason that it is cheap to buy, easy to store and effective to use. It is generally available in two forms – in lumps of varying sizes and as briquettes.

**Wood charcoal pieces.** These have been made in a kiln from various woods. They light fairly easily but because of the variety of origin, they can give off sparks or impart a slight resinous flavour to the food. The pieces burn about twice as fast as briquettes and therefore you will need more for your fire.

**Charcoal briquettes.** These are usually made from hardwood, turned into charcoal and compressed into briquette form. Occasionally they are made from a mixture of charcoal and coal waste. Where dense hardwoods with a low resin content – such as oak, beech and birch – have been used in the manufacture, the briquettes give off very few sparks and burn evenly for a long time. The heat is uniform and intense, without flame, which is necessary for successful barbecue grilling. If you intend to do a lot of barbecuing, it is more economical to buy the briquettes in large quantities, but always store the surplus in a dry place.

**Wood.** The idea of using wood alone for a barbecue is romantic, but not on the whole very practical, since it is not always easy to get enough hardwood or good quality fruitwood to make a satisfactory fire. If you use softwood, you will find that the fire burns too fast and the resin content causes it to flare easily and give off a great deal of smoke. The food will be charred on the outside and underdone in the middle, and the barbecue will not be a great success, however much you enjoy a pleasant bonfire smell.

**Gas.** Liquid butane or propane gas is normally used for a gas-fired barbecue. It is supplied in a cylinder which fits on to the barbecue and the gas passes to a burner at the base of the fire pan. The pan contains lava rock or man-made equivalent which is heated by the gas flame and lets out heat similar to that of burning charcoal.

## LIGHTING THE FIRE

**Firelighters.** For many newcomers to the delights of barbecuing, lighting the fire seems to hold all sorts of terrors. I suppose they have visions of box upon box of discarded matches, leading eventually to an ignominious retreat to the kitchen and the familiar reassurance of the kitchen stove. Really, they have very little to worry about. It is possible to buy self-igniting briquettes (if you are in a complete flap about the fire), which are charcoal briquettes impregnated with a special lighting agent. All you do is put a match to them and hey presto, your fire is on its way.

I always use ordinary household firelighters. You can buy barbecue lighters, which are exactly the same as the household sort but have a different labelling on the box. The firelighters consist of petroleum distillate and urea formaldehyde compressed into a solid white block, which is easily broken into bits or crumbled. Two to three firelighters are sufficient for a large barbecue. Simply break them into small pieces and place among the charcoal. They burn with a flame but soon get the charcoal going. The slight petrol smell disappears when the lighters are burnt out, by which time the charcoal should be burning steadily.

Firelighters also come in granulated form. You sprinkle the granules among the briquettes or pieces of charcoal and light them with a match or taper.

A clean, certain method of starting the fire is to use a portable electric fire-starter. This looks rather like the element in an electric kettle. You place it near the bottom of your pile of briquettes, switch on and leave it for five to ten minutes. You can then take it away and switch off, leaving the charcoal to build up to the required temperature.

A gas blow-lamp is another effective means of lighting the fire. Hold the lamp so that the fire-jet passes easily over the briquettes and wait until they are alight before removing the lamp. The blow-lamp should be held as nearly upright as possible, even if it means crouching down until you are level with the fire.

But for me the firelighters do the trick best.

**Time taken in lighting.** This nearly always seems to take longer than most people expect. Charcoal burns slowly and flame-free, so that it can be hard to tell just how hot it has become. When the lumps or briquettes of charcoal are ready for cooking, they should have what appears to be a film of white ash over the surface. Don't make the mistake of having too much fuel – a common error of those who have never barbecued before. Start with a small pile of briquettes, then spread them out in the fire pan with long-handled tongs so that they form a single layer. If you pile a whole lot more on top, you are just being wasteful.

Remember that good ventilation is needed to make the charcoal burn successfully. If the barbecue has a damper, make sure that it is open, so that there is good bottom draught. Ignition in fire pans which are solid will be easier if you build a fire bed. This is simply a level layer of charcoal underbase, sand or gravel in the fire box which allows the air to pass through it and gives the charcoal the draught it needs. Charcoal underbase absorbs grease and reduces flare and I find it the best. Sand is good but not easily available. Inevitably, the gravel will collect ashes and grease, but it can be washed and used again, provided that it is allowed to dry out properly. If you suspect that there is insufficient draught to get the charcoal burning, a pair of bellows helps. The only trouble with bellows is that they blow the fine ash about and everything within range, including the food itself if you have already started cooking, will soon become covered.

**Ready to cook.** There is a good test to see whether the charcoal is ready for cooking. Hold the palm of your hand over the fire at roughly the height the food will be and count slowly. If you have to pull your hand away at a count of one, the fire is hot; three represents medium heat; and five a low heat. Generally speaking, it takes about 45 minutes for the charcoal to reach a high heat. After dark, the charcoal will appear to be glowing red.

Gas barbecues, however, take much less time to heat up, say five minutes. I have been using one which is fitted with two controls, low and high, and this gives tremendous control over the heat. There is no need to pre-cook any meat, even for a crowd. A great favourite with the family is large chicken legs which on a gas barbecue at low heat take about 25 minutes to reach perfection. They need turning once.

**Keeping the fire going.** Have fresh charcoal or briquettes handy and always add them to the edge of the fire. Never pile them on top. Sudden flare-ups, caused perhaps by fat dripping on to the coals, can be controlled by using a laundry spray or barbecue dowser. Don't dowse the fire – just a quick squirt should be quite sufficient. *Beware* – a laundry spray is very tempting for naughty boys, or girls for that matter, to squirt at each other. I keep mine firmly at my side.

**Aromatic fires.** Usually just the sight of a barbecue is enough to start the mouth watering, but a pleasant smoky smell is the best appetiser of all. By smoky, I don't mean the sort of smoke that comes from fat dripping into the fire, but the aromatic smoke given off by some hardwoods and fruitwoods.

It is possible to buy smoke chips or hickory chips which you should sprinkle (sparingly) on top of the fire. Alternatively, place green sprigs on the fire. Fresh herbs, such as rosemary, marjoram or thyme, placed on the coals, will pass on their flavour to the food. They do this quite quickly and should therefore be added to the fire towards the end of cooking time.

**Varying the heat.** For ordinary barbecues without controls, the simplest way of altering the heat is to move the grill up or down. The closer to the fire it is, the faster the food will cook. If the height of your grill cannot be altered, then move the food to one side. The hottest part of the grill is in the middle.

**Putting the fire out.** If the fire is put out as soon as the cooking is finished, you can use the same coals a second time. Covered barbecues are the easiest in this respect as you just have to close the dampers at the top and bottom. However, much the same effect can be achieved by keeping handy a metal bucket with a close fitting lid. Using a long-handled shovel, you simply transfer the hot coals to the bucket, put on the lid and leave them to cool. Alternatively, you can shovel the coals into a bucket of water – a very quick method – but they must be left to dry out thoroughly before you use them again. Don't pour water on to the barbecue itself for fear of damaging or warping the metal.

## CLEANING AND CARING FOR THE BARBECUE

**Methods of cleaning.** Quite the easiest barbecue to clean is the gas type. All you have to do is to turn it up high for about five minutes with the lid down (if it has one). The bits sticking to the grid burn to a fine dust, which can be removed with a stiff wire brush. I used to borrow one from the workshop for this purpose, but special barbecue brushes are now made. When all the black dust has been loosened, a quick wipe with a damp cloth completes the task.

Ordinary barbecues are a bit more difficult. The best tip I can give is to clean the racks straight after use, even if it means leaving your guests to amuse themselves. Have ready a large sink, filled with hot water to which a biological soap powder has been added, and plunge the racks straight in. It is most effective if you can abandon them to soak overnight, but this can be tiresome if the sink you use is the only one you have. In that case, try leaving them to soak until the end of the party. The longer they can soak, however, the better. Then (wearing rubber gloves because the detergent can play havoc with your hands) clean the base of the grill thoroughly with a pan scourer or brush and rinse well. If you can't face this job, just brush the hot shelves straight after use with a wire brush to remove the burnt remains and leave it at that – I must admit it's what I do!

Cleaning the pan part of the barbecue is easier if you line it with a double layer of foil before the party begins, but for those who may have forgotten to do this, the soaking method is the only alternative. After soaking, dry well.

All the tools should be soaked too. Use a large jug containing a solution of hot water and soapless detergent, so that just the metal parts and not the handles are in the water. I find that a dose of this treatment will loosen the sticky, burnt-on fat sufficiently for it to come off easily.

**Storage.** The racks and pans of a permanent outdoor barbecue should be removable, so that they can be put away for the winter. In summer, it probably won't matter too much if they stay out all the time. Make certain they are clean before wrapping them and putting them away. If you intend to store them in a shed or garage, cover all metal areas with a film of oil to stop them from rusting.

Portable barbecues and the ones on wheels should be similarly treated. A little extra time spent in preparation for storage will add years to the life of your barbecue, however tedious the job may seem.

SAFETY FIRST

**Rules for safety.** With a barbecue, you are literally playing with fire and all basic safety precautions should be meticulously taken. Draw up a list of safety rules, if necessary, and make certain that every member of the family reads them, knows them and will remember them.

Lighting the fire is the time when accidents can most easily happen. It is very tempting, if the fire is a bit slow to get started – perhaps the weather is damp or there is not enough draught – to 'hurry it along a little'. Be firm and resist all such suggestions. *Never*, for example, use petrol, kerosene, lighter fluid, naphtha or any volatile fuel. They are extremely dangerous and also give the food a nasty taste. It is better to hold the barbecue another night if the weather is wrong. A disappointment can be got over quite quickly; a bad burn takes a long time.

Make sure that the barbecue is situated away from overhanging trees and that it is absolutely stable on its legs. I have already mentioned the wisdom of having paving underfoot near the barbecue so that there is no danger at all of slipping.

Use long-handled tools and wear oven gloves when having to handle parts of the barbecue.

**Children.** All children love barbecues and long to do it themselves. My own three are all quite small and no different from the rest, so we have made a rule that they only barbecue under supervision and have to don oven gloves if they so much as approach the fire. Most children are sensible enough to appreciate the reason for these precautions.

Older children, of course, may get resentful if they feel that an anxious parent is forever hovering around. The best way round this is to brief them thoroughly on safety and site the barbecue where they can be discreetly observed – within sight of the kitchen window, for instance.

If all precautions are observed, the most that is likely to happen is a burn on the finger or arm from accidentally touching the hot grill. So have the first-aid kit near at hand, and remember that the quickest and most effective treatment for a burn is to put the affected part into cold water at once, in order to lower the temperature and keep the damage to the minimum. The finger or arm should be kept in the water until the pain stops.

BARBECUE EXTRAS

Once you get hooked on barbecuing, there are all sorts of accessories available. You may improvise to start with, but

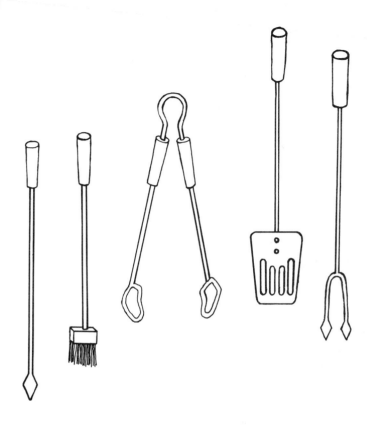

once you acquire them you will wonder how you ever managed without.

**Tongs.** Long-handled tongs are essential for rearranging the coals once they are hot. You may want to concentrate the heat in the centre of the grill or to move hot coals away from dripping fat. Ordinary fire tongs will do if you don't want to spend the money on a special set for the barbecue. Cooking tongs may be used for shifting chops or sausages, etc., turning them over and transferring them to plates.

**Protective clothing.** A general purpose apron with a bib is useful and so are gloves; either oven gloves or asbestos mitts. Keep a number of pairs of gloves near the barbecue when children are involved, so that they may put them on when they want to help you.

**Long-handled fork.** This is used for testing food to see if it is done and for removing pieces when they are cooked. Some people find a fork easier to handle than tongs. A long-handled spatula is useful too for turning food.

**Skewers.** Used for kebabs. Choose long ones, preferably with insulated handles and heat guards. If you have a fitting for a spit, it is possible to get one with an attachment for kebab skewers.

**Spit.** The ideal way of cooking whole chickens or large pieces of meat, a spit is something most barbecue fanatics start to hanker for after a while. If you do decide to get one, I recommend that you buy a spit motor at the same time. The motor fits on to one end of the spit and is usually powered by a low voltage battery. The trouble with a non-motorised spit is that someone has to be detailed to turn it from time to time, or even to hold it in position. If a spit has no locking device, it will always settle with the heaviest part of the meat at the bottom, which results in one half of the chicken getting over cooked while the other half remains practically raw. A motor rotates the spit at intervals, ensuring even cooking and leaving you and other members of the family free to concentrate on other things.

Spits are available with attachments. Apart from the kebab skewer fitting mentioned above, there is a revolving grill basket in which small pieces of meat or vegetables can be placed. They tumble about as the spit revolves. A flat basket can also be bought. This holds fish or other delicate food firmly in place while the spit is turning.

**Fish-smoker.** Smoking your own fish is the ultimate in outdoor cooking luxury and it is possible to buy a special fish-smoker for the purpose. It consists of a smoke box, into which you place a handful of smoking chips, a dripping cover and a grid. Put foil on top of the dripping cover and place it over the smoking chips, standing the grid on top. Gut, clean and dry the fish and put them on the grid. The smoke box goes on top of a fuel container filled with methylated spirits and the whole stands within the shelter of a wind-shield. You just light the fuel and wait for the fish – trout, herring, mackerel, etc. – to become nicely smoked.

**Long-handled basting brush.** Essential for basting food while it is cooking. If a special marinade has been used for things like kebabs, it is useful to be able to keep coating the kebabs with the sauce while they are cooking.

**Thermometer.** A meat thermometer takes the guesswork out of cooking large joints. It should be inserted into the centre of the meat to find out whether the middle is properly done. Take care not to insert the thermometer so that the end touches the spit or bone, which will give a false reading. If the end lies in a pocket of fat, the reading will be too low.

**Foil.** This may be used to line the fire pan and the hood of the barbecue if there is one. Use it in cooking to wrap individual pieces of fish, meat or vegetables. I usually wrap food in two layers of foil for added strength. For those who have a spit, foil has a very useful third purpose – making a drip pan. Unless you have the sort of barbecue which can be turned on its side to allow spit-cooking in front of the fire, some form of drip pan is required underneath the spit to catch the drips which would otherwise fall on the hot coals and cause flare-ups. Ideally use a shallow, oblong foil dish or two equal strips of 18 in. (45 cm) foil folded in half with which you can make the pan. Simply bend up the sides so that they project about $1-1\frac{1}{2}$ in. ($2\frac{1}{2}-3\frac{1}{2}$ cm) and fold the corners to make them leak-proof. It helps to get the corners square if you use a block of wood or small box when folding the sides. The finished pan is then placed immediately under the meat on the spit and the burning coals built up around it. The juices can be used in making gravy. Foil in the fire pan with charcoal underbase and briquettes on top acts as a heat reflector for more economical cooking and makes it easy to clean the barbecue instantly after use.

**Pots and pans.** Most people prefer barbecue food that has been cooked directly on the fire. Nevertheless, there are times when it is useful to cook in a pan, *i.e.* for barbecued baked beans, and sauces. For this purpose, choose thick heavy pans which can withstand the immense heat of the fire and make sure that they are fitted with long handles. Avoid handles made of plastic, which will melt, and loop handles which will get too hot to hold.

**Kitchen paper.** This has a thousand-and-one uses, from mopping up spills to wiping greasy fingers. Always keep a roll handy.

**Wooden board.** Some barbecues have a serving shelf, but you will still need something on which food can be prepared or chopped up. One or two hardwood chopping boards, supported on a firm base, will prove invaluable.

**Plates and cutlery.** Some form of plate is necessary, although people will disagree on whether you need cutlery as well. Unless you want to risk breakages, it is better not to use the household china. Disposable paper plates are ideal for barbecues, but if you do a lot of barbecuing it may be cheaper in the long run to buy plastic picnic plates. The same goes for cutlery – keep a supply of inexpensive, plastic picnic knives and forks in the barbecue box. And for fingers-only barbecues, have plenty of absorbent paper napkins or kitchen tissue handy.

**Sharp knives.** Necessary for preparation – you can keep a variety especially for use with barbecues or borrow the ones from the kitchen.

**Trolley.** Everything has to be taken from its storage place in the house to the barbecue site, and to save countless treks between the two, you may care to invest in a trolley. When I say invest, I mean you can go out and spend a lot of money on a special trolley and this will do the job supremely well, but it *is* possible to improvise.

Some friends of mine, whose children are past the pram stage, have turned their youngest child's old pram into a general carting trolley. It is perfect for carrying oil, brushes, plates, food, bottles and all the rest of the gear. Not only is it very capacious, but the size of the wheels and the springing give it more stability and manoeuvreability over rough ground than a conventional trolley. The pram can be jazzed up a bit by removing the hood and painting the bodywork a bright colour. If you have a wire shopping tray underneath, leave it in place – it makes an extra shelf for cloths, cans, etc.

A really clever handyman could turn an old pram into a truly luxurious hostess trolley.

**Bellows.** Only necessary if the fire simply won't burn without help. A small pair is quite adequate.

# PLANNING A PARTY

There are many occasions when a barbecue party is the ideal entertainment, as the barbecue season extends well over half the year. From Easter and the May Day holiday to Hallowe'en and Guy Fawkes, it is easy to find an excuse for a barbecue celebration, even if it's only Sunday brunch or a picnic party.

Like any other social occasion, success depends on forward planning so that there are no last-minute panics to spoil the day.

**Setting the scene.** Barbecues may be casual affairs, but the best casual atmosphere is one that has been set with care. With large parties especially, guests appreciate the feeling that their hosts have gone to some trouble; it is only with old and close friends that the hostess can greet them with charcoal smudges on her nose and the grubby jeans she wears when washing the dog.

The easiest way of getting the atmosphere right from the start is to plan around a theme: it could be historical – Ancient Greek, for example, with jugs of wine and large bowls of fruit, or Tudor, with mead to drink and whole chickens roasting on the spit; alternatively, try Western, with hamburgers and beans, or Mediterranean seafront, with fish and bottles of plonk.

Lights will transform even the most ordinary garden. If you can't run a string of coloured light-bulbs around the trees, try placing candles in jam jars and hanging them from branches or burying nightlights in shallow containers in the flower beds.

**The menu.** Make it simple, particularly if you have invited a lot of people. Have a choice of meats – say, chicken and American beefburgers or lamb kebabs – and serve them with a straightforward salad and French bread, with fruit and ice cream to follow. Barbecue sauces can be provided in small bowls for guests to help themselves at will.

When assessing the amount you will need, remember that people eating in the open tend to have hearty appetites and allow $1\frac{1}{2}$ to 2 portions per person. *One* portion is approximately four ounces of meat – *i.e.* one chicken piece, a large chop or beefburger or two sausages. Each person will probably manage one bread roll or two slices of French bread, two or more glasses of cold drink and one cup of coffee.

The really ambitious hostess might consider offering a whole roasted saddle of lamb or suckling pig, both of which should ideally be cooked on a spit and take approximately three hours for the saddle and five hours for the suckling pig to reach perfection. The saddle of lamb will need basting while it is cooking, but the pig not. Instead, score the skin and rub it with salt to make the crackling crisp. A saddle of lamb is sufficient for about 10 people, a suckling pig for about 20, but remember that you will need a skilled person to carve and facilities for keeping meat hot. The cooking time will very much depend on the intensity of heat.

The best way of keeping things hot is to have a spare barbecue alongside the main one (meat-tins lined with foil serve this purpose admirably). Cold things can be kept cold by placing them in insulated boxes complete with ice packs. Chill salads beforehand for several hours in the refrigerator and they will stay cool for a long time. It is best when cooking for large numbers, for meats such as sausages and chicken pieces to be pre-cooked in the ordinary oven or microwave oven. Do this the night before or early on the morning of the party and keep them, covered, in the refrigerator until needed. Then brown them on the barbecue.

**Cooking and serving.** Two large tables, or more according to numbers, will ease the cooking and serving problems. One should be covered with a plastic cloth and equipped with wooden chopping boards and used for barbecued food, bread and any uncooked meats. The other, nearby, can carry salad, puddings, and things like plates, cutlery and serving spoons. A drinks table will also be needed, placed well apart from the other two to prevent congestion.

**Getting rid of rubbish.** It is best to use paper or plastic plates and cups for a crowd. If you choose the former, make certain that there are large boxes dotted around for the rubbish. If you can keep empty tins and waste paper in separate boxes, the tins can go straight into the dustbin as soon as the box is full, while the other box can be burned next day on the bonfire.

Another point to remember is to provide some sort of receptacle for cigarette ends. Although fewer people seem to smoke these days, there are always some who do and they may well hesitate to grind out their cigarettes on the patio paving or fling them into the flower beds. Metal buckets or old biscuit tins half-filled with sand make convenient and safe outdoor ashtrays. They can be dotted about wherever people are sitting or standing.

Finally, there is the weather. If your patio is half-covered, you are in a strong position and the weather prospects won't worry you. But never hold a barbecue in a completely enclosed area because of the danger from charcoal fumes. At least the whole of one side of the area should be open.

# HOW TO BUY AND COOK THE BASIC MEAT AND POULTRY

## Buying hints

*Meat.* Choose first quality tender meat. It is no good buying the cheaper, coarse cuts of meat or boiling fowls for barbecuing as the cooking time is short and therefore the meat would remain tough. I have found that steak and meat tenderising powders add flavour, but in fact don't tenderise the meat. Have the meat trimmed of excess fat where necessary and the joints or pieces cut in uniform shapes and thicknesses in the case of steaks.

*Fish.* This should be really fresh and preferably on the bone or whole. I find the best to barbecue are trout, mackerel, large sardines and steaks of sea bass or salmon.

## Cooking times for each side

All meat for barbecuing should be already at room temperature, so remove it from the fridge at least an hour before cooking. The times are very approximate as it depends on the efficiency of the barbecue, the intensity of the heat and the number of portions being cooked. One steak will take less time than six cooked at the same time on a small barbecue.

Cooking times given in minutes below on chart.

|  | Rare | Well done | Comments |
|---|---|---|---|
| *Beef* | | | |
| Steaks ½ in. thick | 3 | 8 | Beef is best served rare or underdone. |
| Steak 1 in. thick | 5 | 10 | |
| Beefburgers 1 in. thick | 4 | 7 | Always use good quality mince when making your own. |
| *Lamb* | | | |
| Loin chops | 5 | 10 | Lamb may be served slightly pink if preferred. |
| Chump chops | 6 | 12 | |
| Cutlets | 4 | 7 | |
| Leg of lamb, on the spit | allow 30 minutes per lb | | Best boned and rolled. |
| Kebabs | 7 | 10–15 | If the meat is liked well done, thread the pieces loosely on the skewers; if under done, push close together. |
| *Pork* | | | |
| Chops | | 13 | Pork should always be well done. |
| *Sausages* | | | |
| Large | | 15 | No need to prick sausages; always turn frequently. |
| Chipolata | | 10 | |
| *Chicken* | | | |
| Legs | | 25 | Chicken is cooked if the thickest part is pierced with a skewer and the juices run out clear. |
| Wings | | 20 | |
| Whole on a spit | allow 30 minutes per lb | | |
| *Fish* | | | |
| Whole | | 10–12 | Do not over cook or the fish will be dry. |
| Steaks 1 in. thick | | 3–5 | |
| Sardines | | 8–10 | Leave heads and tails on and coat in sea salt. |

# Variety Recipes

## Barbecued Chicken Drumsticks
for eight

*Sauce*
1 rounded tablespoon apricot jam
1 tablespoon Worcestershire sauce
3 tablespoons tomato ketchup
1 tablespoon soy sauce
1 level teaspoon Dijon mustard
pinch cayenne pepper
1 large clove garlic, crushed

salt and pepper
8 chicken drumsticks

Pre-heat the barbecue.

Blend all the sauce ingredients together thoroughly. Season the drumsticks and brush the sauce over them.

Oil the grill, lay the drumsticks on it and grill over a medium grill for 20 minutes, turning regularly and brushing with more sauce during the cooking. The time will vary with the size and thickness of the drumsticks, but chicken is cooked if the thickest part of drumstick is pierced with a skewer and the juices come out clear. If they are bloody, continue cooking for a little longer.

Barbecued Chicken Drumsticks and Savoury Sausage Risotto.

## Devilled Chicken Joints

serves four, but this recipe is easy to adjust to coat any number of chicken joints

2 tablespoons paprika pepper
1 level teaspoon garlic powder
1 level teaspoon salt
4 chicken joints
oil

Pre-heat the barbecue and oil the grill.

Blend all the dry ingredients together and brush over the chicken joints.

Place the chicken on the oiled grill, bone side down, and grill over a medium grill for 20–25 minutes, turning once during cooking and brushing with a little more oil.

# Chicken Lyonnaise

*For each portion allow*
1 chicken joint
salt and pepper
butter
1 medium potato, sliced
1 small onion, finely sliced
chopped fresh herbs

Heat the oven to 375°F (190°C), gas 5.

Place the chicken in a dish, season well and dot with butter. Mix the potato and onion together and put in a shallow dish, season and dot with butter. Cook both dishes in the oven for about 45 minutes or until the chicken and vegetables are tender, basting occasionally.

Taking a double-thickness square of foil, lay a portion of vegetables in the centre, put the chicken joint on top and pour over any juices left from the cooking. Sprinkle with the herbs.

Fold over the foil and seal the edges. When required, heat through on a moderate-to-hot grill for about 15 minutes, depending on the number of foil parcels. If you are heating a lot, the ones in the centre will be done before the outside parcels and it is a good idea to move them around on the grill so that all the food is ready at the same time.

This recipe is ideal for a crowd. It is cooked in advance and may then be re-heated on the barbecue when required. Vary the sizes of the chicken – small pieces of wings for children and the large legs for grown ups.

## Barbecued Chicken Parcels
for four

2 oz (50 g) butter
4 chicken portions
1 small onion, finely chopped
4 tablespoons tomato ketchup
2 tablespoons vinegar
2 level tablespoons mango chutney, chopped
1 tablespoon Worcestershire sauce
¼ teaspoon French mustard
1 teaspoon sugar

Heat 1 oz (25 g) butter in a frying pan and fry the chicken portions until brown on both sides. Lift out and place each portion on a lightly buttered double-thickness square of foil.

Add the remaining butter to the pan and fry the onion gently until tender, without browning. Add the remaining ingredients to the pan and bring to the boil, spooning a little of the sauce over each piece of chicken. Close the foil carefully at the sides and ends to seal in the juices.

Pre-heat the barbecue and cook the chicken for 30–40 minutes over a moderate grill, turning two or three times. The cooking time will vary with the thickness and size of the joints, legs taking longer than wings. Serve on plain boiled rice with the juices poured over.

This is an ideal recipe for a crowd as it is easily adapted to any number of portions and may be prepared in advance.

## Marinated Indian Chicken
for four

4 tablespoons thin honey
1 level tablespoon curry powder
1 level teaspoon salt
1 level teaspoon French mustard
4 chicken legs

Blend the honey, curry powder, salt and mustard together. Lay the chicken legs in a single layer in a dish and pour over the honey mixture. Cover the dish and leave in the refrigerator overnight, or for at least eight hours.

Pre-heat the barbecue and oil the grill.

Spoon the marinade over the chicken to coat thoroughly and then cook over a moderate-to-low grill for 20–25 minutes, turning two or three times during cooking, so that the chicken gets evenly cooked through without the skin becoming too brown. Brush with a little of the marinade during cooking.

## Lamburgers
makes eight

1 finely chopped onion
1 oz (25 g) butter
1 lb (400 g) lean minced lamb
1 finely chopped stick celery
1 tablespoon tomato purée
1 tablespoon tomato ketchup
1 teaspoon mixed herbs
salt and pepper
2 oz (50 g) white breadcrumbs
8 soft rolls

Fry the onion gently in the butter, and mix with the remaining ingredients. Divide the mixture and shape into eight burgers.

Pre-heat the barbecue and oil a burger mesh.

Brush lamburgers with 'No Cook' Barbecue Baste (see page 61) and grill over a medium grill for about 15 minutes,

turning once and basting with the sauce during cooking.
Serve in split rolls.

Lamburgers, Lamb Chops and Jacket Potatoes.

## Lamb Chops Ratatouille
for four

1 small aubergine
4 courgettes
salt
2 oz (50 g) butter
2 medium onions, sliced
1 green pepper
1 red pepper
1 clove garlic
¾ lb (300 g) tomatoes
ground black pepper
4 lamb chops

Cut the aubergine and courgettes into ½ in. (1.25 cm) slices, put on kitchen paper, sprinkle with salt and leave for 30 minutes.

Heat the butter in a pan, add the onions and cook slowly until they are soft but not coloured.

Remove the seeds from the peppers and cut into thin strips.

Pre-heat the barbecue.

Dry the aubergine and courgettes carefully with more kitchen paper, add them to the pan with the peppers and garlic and cover and simmer gently for 30 minutes, stirring occasionally.

Put the tomatoes in a bowl, cover with boiling water and leave to stand for 10 seconds. Drain them, then peel, quarter and remove the seeds. Add to the pan and cook for 10 minutes. Taste and adjust seasoning, then turn into a foil dish and put on the barbecue.

Trim any excess fat from the chops and brown them on both sides over a moderate grill. Then lay them on top of the ratatouille and cook for about 20 minutes until the chops are tender – the time will vary with the thickness of the meat.

**Lamb Noisettes**
makes six noisettes

6 cutlet pieces best end of neck of lamb
salt and pepper
dried rosemary
3 lamb's kidneys

Pre-heat the barbecue and oil the grill.

Ask the butcher to bone the best end of neck for you. Alternatively, it is simple to do yourself: cut off the thick chine bone at the thick end of the joint and trim away all excess fat from the meat. Using a sharp pointed knife, cut along either side of each bone and ease it out.

Season the meat well and sprinkle with rosemary. Remove the skin and cores from the kidneys and lay along the width of the meat. Roll up the joint lengthwise and tie at 1 in. (2.5 cm) intervals with fine string. Cut the joint into six even slices, securing each slice with two fine skewers to make sure that the kidney will not pop out during cooking.

Grill over a moderate grill for about 10–15 minutes, turning once.

Rather special and different for entertaining, they take time to prepare, but are worth it.

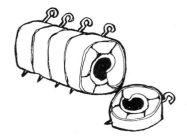

Variety with Lamb – Lamb Kebabs, Lamburgers and Lamb Chops.

## Greek Meatballs
makes about 25–30 meatballs

1 lb (400 g) lean minced lamb
2 oz (50 g) semolina
3 tablespoons Worcestershire sauce
1 level teaspoon salt
¼ level teaspoon dried marjoram
ground black pepper
2 cloves garlic, crushed

Pre-heat the barbecue and brush the grill with oil.

Mix all the ingredients together and knead to a firm mixture. Shape into small balls, 1 in. (2.5 cm) in diameter, using wetted palms.

Lightly oil metal skewers and thread on the meatballs. Brush with Spicy Tomato Baste (see page 60) and grill over a medium grill for 10 minutes, basting twice with the sauce and turning during cooking.

## American Beefburgers
makes eight beefburgers

¾ lb (300 g) best raw minced beef
½ lb (200 g) pork sausage meat
1 medium onion, grated
1 level teaspoon salt
ground black pepper
1 rounded teaspoon chopped fresh herbs

Pre-heat the barbecue and oil the grill.

Place all the ingredients together in a bowl and mix thoroughly until well blended. Lightly flour hands and roll the mixture into eight balls, flattening each out to a 3 in. (7.5 cm) beefburger.

Grill on the barbecue for about eight minutes, turning once or until cooked through. Serve in soft bread rolls with a spoonful of Tomato Bennett sauce (see page 61).

## Beefburgers Cordon Bleu
makes four beefburgers

1 lb (400 g) lean minced beef
1 teaspoon Worcestershire sauce
1 level teaspoon fresh chopped marjoram
1 level teaspoon salt
ground black pepper
4 slices Cheddar cheese

Pre-heat the barbecue and oil the grill.

Blend the beef, Worcestershire sauce, marjoram and seasoning together.

Lightly flour hands and roll the mixture into eight balls, flattening each out to 3 in. (7.5 cm) diameter beefburgers. Sandwich the beefburgers together in pairs with a slice of Cheddar cheese in the centre.

Put the beefburgers on the grill and cook over a medium grill for about 10 minutes, turning once or until the beefburgers are cooked through and the cheese in the centre has started to melt.

Serve the beefburgers as they are or, for those who are very hungry, they may be put inside a split soft bread roll.

## Pork Sausages

1 lb (400 g) large pork sausages
1 lb (400 g) pork chipolatas

Pre-heat the barbecue, then brush the grill with oil.

Lay all the sausages on the grill (no need to prick) and cook over a medium grill, for about 15 minutes for the large sausages and 10 minutes for the chipolatas.

Serve with Mustard Mayonnaise (see page 67), Cranberry Dip (page 65) or Piquant Sauce (page 64).

**Frankfurter Rolls**
makes eight rolls

1 packet (8) frankfurter sausages
8 slices ham
a little German mustard
melted butter
8 long soft bread rolls

Pre-heat the barbecue and oil the grill.

Cook the frankfurter sausages as directed on the packet and leave to cool.

Spread each slice of ham with a little mustard. Lay a frankfurter sausage on each slice and roll up. Put the ham rolls side by side in a line and thread a long skewer through all eight at each end (this makes cooking and turning very much easier).

Brush with a little melted butter and grill for about five minutes, turning over a moderate grill until the rolls are warmed through.

Push the ham and frankfurters off the skewers and serve each one in a split soft bread roll.

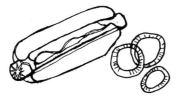

## Gammon with Honey and Orange
for four

4 gammon steaks
3 tablespoons thin honey
1 tablespoon Dijon mustard
1 orange

Pre-heat the barbecue and oil the grill.

Trim any excess fat from the gammon steaks. Blend the honey with the mustard and brush over the gammon. Grill over a moderate-to-low barbecue for 10–12 minutes, turning two or three times during cooking and brushing with a little more honey so that the gammon becomes evenly brown.

Cut a thin slice from the top and bottom of the orange and then cut it into four slices. Lay them flat on a square of foil, seal and put on the edge of the barbecue while cooking the gammon.

Serve the gammon with a slice of orange on top of each steak. This is delicious served with a green salad and jacket potatoes.

## Savoury Bacon Rolls
makes 24 rolls

12 rashers streaky bacon
12 soaked stoned prunes
12 chicken livers
melted butter

Pre-heat the barbecue and oil the grill.

Cutting the rind from the bacon rashers stretch each rasher flat with the back of a knife; then cut each one in half. Wrap each piece of bacon around a prune or chicken liver.

Lightly oil long skewers and thread on the bacon rolls. Brush with a little melted butter and grill over a hot grill for about six minutes, turning once. When cooked, ease them off the skewers with a fork and pile into a bowl. Leave people to help themselves – if liked the rolls may be speared with a cocktail stick.

## Brochettes of Liver

makes four brochettes

½ lb (200 g) lamb's liver
1 tablespoon oil
3 tablespoons red wine
small clove garlic, crushed
½ teaspoon brown sugar
salt and pepper
1 teaspoon Worcestershire sauce
4 oz (100 g) button mushrooms, washed

Trim the liver, cut into 1 in. (2.5 cm) squares and put in a dish. Blend the oil, wine, garlic, sugar, salt, pepper and Worcestershire sauce together and pour over the liver, cover and leave to marinade for three hours.

Pre-heat the barbecue and oil the grill.

Thread pieces of liver and mushrooms alternately on oiled skewers and grill over a medium grill for six to eight minutes, basting with the marinade and turning during cooking. Serve with rice and a green salad.

# KEBABS

I find it best to barbecue all meat and onion together on skewers and most vegetable kebabs separately as the vegetable cooking time is shorter.

## Bacon, Kidney and Sausage Kebabs
makes four kebabs

6 rashers streaky bacon
4 chipolata sausages
4 lamb's kidneys
*Baste*
1 teaspoon tomato ketchup
1 teaspoon Worcestershire sauce
1 tablespoon corn oil

Pre-heat the barbecue and oil the grill.

Remove the rind from the bacon and stretch flat with the back of a knife. Cut each rasher in half and roll up. Twist each sausage into two and separate with a knife. Skin the kidneys, cut in half and remove the cores.

Lightly oil four skewers and on each put three bacon rolls, two pieces of kidney and two small sausages.

Mix the baste ingredients together and brush over the kebabs. Place on the grill and cook for 10–12 minutes over a medium grill, brushing with more baste and turning during cooking.

## Chicken Liver Kebabs
makes four kebabs

2 courgettes
6 oz (150 g) chicken livers
4 oz (100 g) button mushrooms
melted butter

Pre-heat the barbecue and oil the grill.

Wash and thickly slice the courgettes, place in a saucepan, cover with cold water and bring to the boil. Simmer for one minute, then drain thoroughly. This removes the slight acid flavour from the skins.

Trim the chicken livers, removing any pieces of sinews and wash the mushrooms.

Oil four long skewers and thread on the courgettes, chicken livers and mushrooms alternately. Lightly brush with a little melted butter and grill over a moderate grill for 10 minutes, brushing with more butter and turning during cooking.

Serve with rice and tomato sauce.

## Chinese Pork Kebabs
makes four kebabs

2 tablespoons soy sauce
1 teaspoon sugar
2 tablespoons sherry
3 tablespoons water
1 lb (400 g) pork fillet
4 small onions, quartered

Blend the soy sauce, sugar, sherry and water together. Cut the pork fillet into 1 in. (2.5 cm) cubes and put in a dish with the soy sauce mixture. Cover and leave to marinade in a cool place for several hours.

Pre-heat the barbecue and oil the grill.

Thread the meat, alternating with quarters of onion, on four long oiled skewers and grill over a medium grill for about 15 minutes, turning and basting with the marinade during cooking.

## Pork Fruity Kebabs
makes four kebabs

*Baste*
6 oz (150 g) soft brown sugar
4 tablespoons apricot jam
2 tablespoons Worcestershire sauce
6 tablespoons vinegar
1 level teaspoon dry mustard
*Kebabs*
1 lb (400 g) pork fillet or leg of pork
8 oz (200 g) can apricots
8 prunes, soaked and stoned

Pre-heat the barbecue and oil the grill.

Combine all the baste ingredients in a small pan and heat gently until the sugar has dissolved.

Cut the pork into 1 in. (2.5 cm) pieces. Drain the apricots, reserving the juice and arrange the pork, apricots and prunes alternately on four oiled skewers. Brush with the baste and barbecue over a moderate grill for 15 minutes, turning and basting several times during cooking.

Stir the apricot juice into the baste remaining in the saucepan, re-heat, stirring until well blended. Serve the kebabs on plain boiled rice with the sauce poured over.

## Pork and Pineapple Kebabs
makes four kebabs

1 lb (400 g) pork fillet or leg of pork
8 oz (200 g) can pineapple chunks
1 tablespoon lemon juice
1 level tablespoon chopped fresh sage
1 large green pepper

Cut the pork fillet into 1 in. (2.5 cm) cubes trimming off any fat and put in a dish. Drain the juice from the can of pineapple, blend with the lemon juice and sage and pour over the pork, cover and leave to marinade for several hours.

Pre-heat the barbecue and oil the grill.

Cut the green pepper in quarters and remove all the seeds and white pith and then cut into large pieces.

Oil four long skewers and put on the pieces of pork alternating with pineapple chunks and pieces of green pepper. Brush with a little of the marinade and barbecue the kebabs over a moderate grill for 15 minutes, turning and basting several times during the cooking.

## Lamb Kebabs
makes four kebabs

1 lb (400 g) lamb, from leg or shoulder, cut into 1 in. (2.5 cm) cubes
4 tomatoes, cut into quarters
4 oz (100 g) button mushrooms
1 green pepper, deseeded and blanched in boiling water
bay leaves
salt and pepper
*Marinade*
2 tablespoons oil
1 tablespoon vinegar
1 clove garlic, crushed
1 onion, roughly chopped
salt and pepper

Cut the lamb into cubes and soak in the marinade overnight if possible.

Pre-heat the barbecue and oil the grill.

Thread the lamb, tomatoes, mushrooms, green pepper and bay leaves alternately on to four oiled skewers. Season well with salt and pepper.

Cook on a hot grill for eight to ten minutes, turning frequently.

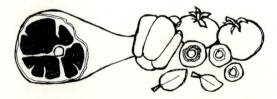

## Fishermen's Kebabs
makes four kebabs

*Baste*
juice of ½ a lemon
1 tablespoon Worcestershire sauce
salt and pepper

*Kebabs*
7 oz (175 g) packet frozen cod steaks
2 oz (50 g) button mushrooms, washed
3 oz (75 g) large, cooked, peeled prawns
4 very small tomatoes

Pre-heat the barbecue and oil the grill.

Blend all the baste ingredients together.

Cut each cod steak into six pieces while still frozen hard. Place on four oiled skewers alternating with mushrooms, prawns and tomatoes. Brush with the baste and cook over a moderate grill for 10–12 minutes, brushing with more baste and turning several times during cooking.

**Salmon Fishcakes**
makes eight fishcakes

8 oz (200 g) can pink salmon
12 oz (300 g) freshly boiled, sieved potatoes
1 tablespoon finely chopped parsley
salt and black pepper

Pre-heat the barbecue.

Drain the salmon, flake the fish and remove any black skin and bones. Put in a bowl with the potatoes, parsley and seasoning and mix thoroughly.

Turn on to a lightly floured board and shape into a roll. Cut into eight even slices and shape into fishcakes with lightly floured hands.

Oil a burger mesh and place four fishcakes in it, close and cook over a moderate grill for eight minutes, turning once. Cook the other fishcakes in the same way. Serve with tomato sauce.

Make these too with less glamorous fish for every day. Always serve with a sauce, and a cucumber and dill salad goes well. No need for potatoes, just French bread crispened up on the barbecue for five minutes.

---

**Fresh Sardines**

Pre-heat the barbecue and oil the grill.

Choose large fresh sardines and clean thoroughly but leave the heads and tails on. Well coat the sardines in a Beleine sea salt. This is not strong and gives the sardines a lovely crisp coating.

Cook over a medium barbecue for about eight to ten minutes, turning.

Serve with wedges of lemon, Maître d'Hôtel butter (see page 71) and a good dressed Tomato and Onion Salad (see page 78).

## Trout with Horseradish Butter
for four

4 rainbow trout
butter
foil
salt and pepper
2 oz (50 g) Horseradish Butter (see page 70)
chopped parsley
4 slices lemon

Pre-heat the barbecue.

Clean the trout, leaving the heads and tails on. Wipe dry and lay each fish on a square of buttered foil. Season well and place $\frac{1}{2}$ oz ($12\frac{1}{2}$ g) Horseradish Butter inside each fish. Sprinkle with the parsley and lay a slice of lemon on each trout.

Close the foil carefully at the sides and ends to seal the juices in while cooking. Place on the barbecue and cook over a moderate grill for about 25 minutes, turning occasionally.

Serve the trout from the foil with all the juices poured over.

## Devilled Mackerel
for four

4 mackerel
butter
foil
2 oz (50 g) Devilled Butter (see page 70)
4 oz (100 g) button mushrooms

Pre-heat the barbecue.

Clean the mackerel and remove the heads. Wipe dry and lay each fish on a piece of buttered foil.

Place $\frac{1}{2}$ oz ($12\frac{1}{2}$ g) Devilled Butter inside each fish with 1 oz (25 g) button mushrooms. Close the foil at the sides and ends to seal in the juices.

Place on a medium barbecue and grill for about 25 minutes, turning occasionally. Serve straight from the parcel with the juice poured over.

## Savoury Sausage Risotto
for four to six

1 oz (25 g) lard
8 oz (200 g) chipolata sausages
1 large onion, chopped
6 oz (150 g) streaky bacon, rind removed, chopped
6 oz (150 g) long-grain rice
1¼ pints (625 ml) beef stock
4 oz (100 g) button mushrooms, quartered
1 small green pepper, seeds removed, cut into rings and blanched
2 tomatoes, skinned and quartered
2 tablespoons Worcestershire sauce
salt and pepper

Heat lard in pan and fry sausages for 10 minutes, turning, until well browned. Drain, cut into 1½ in. (4 cm) lengths, and keep warm. Clean pan, melt butter and fry onion and bacon gently for five minutes.

Add rice and cook for two minutes. Stir in stock, bring to boil, stirring, and simmer gently for 15 minutes.

Add mushrooms and green pepper, reserving a few rings for garnish, and cook for a further 10 minutes, until stock has been absorbed. Stir in tomatoes, Worcestershire sauce, sausages and season to taste. Serve garnished with rings of green pepper.

This is a useful stand-by which can be prepared before the barbecue starts and served as an addition to the barbecued meat.

# Bastes and Sauces etc.

# BASTES

Basting sauces add piquancy and moisture to food, brush on lightly during cooking, any left-over sauce can be served with the food.

## Spicy Tomato Baste

4 tablespoons Worcestershire sauce
¼ pint (125 ml) tomato ketchup
1 level teaspoon made English mustard
2 level tablespoons dark soft brown sugar
4 tablespoons water
1 tablespoon lemon juice

Place all the ingredients together in a saucepan and bring slowly to the boil, stirring until the sugar has dissolved. Simmer for three to four minutes to allow the sauce to thicken.

Use as required as a baste for meatballs, sausages, chops and pieces of chicken. Store in the refrigerator in an airtight container.

## Chinese Basting Sauce

1 very small or pickling onion
1 tablespoon oil
3 tablespoons sherry
3 tablespoons soy sauce
1 tablespoon Worcestershire sauce

Cut the onion in small pieces and press through a garlic press, blend with all the other ingredients.

Use as required. This is delicious brushed over chicken breasts.

## 'No Cook' Barbecue Baste

1 teaspoon chilli powder
1 teaspoon celery salt
2 tablespoons soft brown sugar
2 tablespoons wine vinegar
2 tablespoons Worcestershire sauce
3 tablespoons tomato ketchup
1 small cup stock
tabasco sauce, to taste

Blend all the ingredients together and use as required.

This baste goes especially well with Lamb Kebabs, (see page 54) lamb chops or Lamburgers (page 40).


SAUCES

Sauces can either be hot or cold. My favourites are Tomato Bennett sauce and the Easy Curry Mayonnaise.

## Tomato Bennett Sauce

1 oz (25 g) butter
1 small onion, finely chopped
4 tablespoons tomato ketchup
2 tablespoons vinegar
2 level tablespoons mango chutney, chopped
1 tablespoon Worcestershire sauce
1 teaspoon sugar
$\frac{1}{4}$ teaspoon French mustard

Melt the butter in a small saucepan, add the onion and fry gently until tender without colouring. Add the rest of the ingredients and bring to the boil. Simmer gently for two to three minutes and serve hot or cold with sausages, chops, pieces of chicken or any simply cooked barbecued food.

# Tomato Sauce

1 tablespoon oil
1 rasher streaky bacon, chopped
1 large onion, chopped
1 oz (25 g) flour
14 oz (350 g) can peeled tomatoes
¼ pint (125 ml) chicken stock
1 level teaspoon salt
black pepper
1 tablespoon Worcestershire sauce
1 level teaspoon sugar
1 bay leaf
1 clove garlic, crushed

Heat the oil in a small saucepan and fry the bacon and onion for five minutes. Stir in the flour and cook for a minute. Add the peeled tomatoes and chicken stock and bring to the boil, stirring until thickened. Add the remaining ingredients, cover the saucepan and simmer gently for 20–30 minutes.

Remove the pan from the heat and sieve the sauce. Rinse out the saucepan and return the sauce to the pan. Re-heat, taste and check seasoning.

This is a good sauce to have on the table at a barbecue as it goes well with most barbecued food.

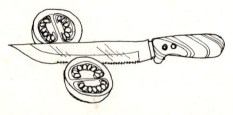

## Barbecue Sauce

1 small onion, very finely chopped
1 stick celery, very finely chopped
1 clove garlic, crushed
1 oz (25 g) butter
2 tablespoons dry mustard
2 tablespoons demerara sugar
½ teaspoon tabasco sauce
1 14 oz (350 g) can tomato juice
2 tablespoons Worcestershire sauce
juice of 1 fresh grapefruit
4 tablespoons wine vinegar
1 bay leaf

Fry the onion, celery and garlic in the butter for five to ten minutes, until the vegetables are soft but not brown.

Add the remaining ingredients and bring to the boil. Simmer for 10–15 minutes.

Remove bay leaf and serve.

This sauce goes well with grilled lamb chops and is sufficient for 16 chops.

## Piquant Sauce

5 tablespoons malt vinegar
1 tablespoon Worcestershire sauce
2 level tablespoons redcurrant jelly
1 level teaspoon made mustard
2 level tablespoons demerara sugar

Place all the ingredients together in a small saucepan and heat gently until all the sugar has dissolved and the redcurrant jelly melted.

Bring to the boil and then boil rapidly for two to three minutes. Remove from the heat, pour into a dish and serve hot with sausages.

Piquant Sauce, Easy Curry Mayonnaise and Tomato Bennett Sauce.

# DIPS

**Cranberry Dip**
for four to six

8½ oz (212 g) jar cranberry sauce
2 rounded teaspoons cornflour
1 tablespoon water
2 teaspoons Worcestershire sauce

Sieve the cranberry sauce into a bowl. Blend together the cornflour, water and Worcestershire sauce in a small saucepan. Stir in the cranberry purée and bring to the boil, stirring. Simmer for two minutes.

Taste and check flavouring and if the sauce seems a little thick, add an extra tablespoon water. Serve hot as a dip for sausages or pieces of chicken.

---

**Savoury Topping**
for six

½ oz (12½ g) butter
½ oz (12½ g) flour
¼ pint (125 ml) milk
4½ oz (113 g) can liver pâté
2 baby dill cucumbers
1 tablespoon mango chutney
salt and pepper

Melt the butter in a small saucepan, stir in the flour and cook for two minutes. Add the milk and bring to the boil, stirring. Simmer for a minute. Stir in the can of liver pâté and mix well until blended, leave to cool.

Finely chop the dill cucumbers and mango chutney and stir into the sauce. Season to taste.

Serve as topping for jacket potatoes or beefburgers.

## Sweetcorn and Bacon Topping

for six to eight, depending on the size of jacket potato

2 oz (50 g) streaky bacon
11½ oz (282 g) can sweetcorn with peppers
3 rounded tablespoons mayonnaise
1 level tablespoon chopped chives
salt and pepper

Remove the rind from the bacon and cut into thin strips. Place in a small pan and fry quickly until golden brown and crisp. Lift out with a slotted spoon and drain on kitchen paper until cold.

Thoroughly drain the sweetcorn, then place in a bowl with the mayonnaise, bacon and chives. Mix well and season to taste. Serve with jacket potatoes.

## Pineapple and Cheese Topping

8 oz (200 g) can pineapple tidbits
8 oz (200 g) carton cottage cheese
a good pinch cayenne pepper
salt

Thoroughly drain the pineapple. Put the cottage cheese into a bowl and stir in the pineapple and cayenne pepper. Taste and check seasoning and add salt to taste.

Serve as a topping for jacket potatoes or as an accompaniment to plain barbecued meats such as chicken or gammon steaks.

## Easy Curry Mayonnaise

½ pint (250 ml) home-made or good bought mayonnaise
1 level teaspoon Dijon mustard
1 level teaspoon curry powder
1 tablespoon finely chopped mango chutney
1 tablespoon lemon juice

Mix all the ingredients together and taste and check if any salt and pepper are necessary.

Store covered in the refrigerator, for 24 hours to allow the flavours to blend.

Serve with sausages, gammon steaks and simply cooked steaks and pork chops.

## Mustard Mayonnaise
for ten

½ pint (250 ml) home-made or good bought mayonnaise
1 rounded teaspoon made mustard
a good pinch curry powder
1 rounded teaspoon tomato purée
freshly ground black pepper
2 tablespoons single cream

Place the mayonnaise in a bowl and stir in the mustard, curry powder, tomato purée and freshly ground black pepper. Taste and check seasoning. Add a little extra mustard if you like a really strong flavour, but remember that the flavours will improve with keeping.

Keep in a refrigerator until required, then stir in the cream and turn into a serving dish or bowl.

This dip is especially good served with hot barbecued pork sausages.

## Tomato Dip

1 medium onion
2 sticks celery
1 oz (50 g) butter
8 oz (200 g) can tomatoes
1 tablespoon Worcestershire sauce
½ level teaspoon sugar
¼ level teaspoon mixed dried herbs
salt
freshly ground black pepper

Very finely chop the onion and thinly slice the celery. Melt the butter in a small saucepan and add the onion and celery and cover and cook over a low heat until soft but not brown. This will take about 10–15 minutes.

Stir in the remaining ingredients and bring to the boil. Then reduce the heat and simmer gently for five minutes. Taste and check seasoning.

Serve hot as a dip for sausages, or pieces of plain chicken, or put a spoonful on top of a beefburger.

## Soured Cream Topping for Potatoes
makes sufficient topping for about six potatoes

¼ pint (125 ml) soured cream
1 rounded teaspoon fresh chopped chives
freshly ground black pepper

Turn the soured cream into a small bowl and stir in the chives and plenty of pepper. Cover and leave in a cool place for the flavours to blend for about an hour.

Serve a spoonful on top of a jacket potato.

# MARINADES

Marinades tenderise the meat and add to the flavour too. Worcestershire sauce, wine, vinegar and lemon juice give the tenderising agent to marinades.

Ideally leave the food to marinade in a plastic, glass or china container, covered in the refrigerator for 24 hours. Never use a metal container as it would affect the flavour.

Once meat has been marinated, reduce the marinade by boiling until it reaches coating consistency. Then use on the barbecue as a baste to brush on the meat. If you want a sauce, just heat and serve with the food without reducing.

## Fresh Herb Marinade

2 tablespoons oil
4 tablespoons lemon juice
1 clove garlic, crushed
finely sliced onion
1 level teaspoon chopped fresh thyme
1 level teaspoon chopped fresh marjoram
1 level teaspoon chopped fresh parsley

Place all the ingredients together in a small bowl and mix thoroughly. The marinade may also be prepared by putting the ingredients in a screw topped jar, shaking until well blended. Store in the refrigerator and use as required.

## Red Wine Marinade

2 tablespoons oil
6 tablespoons red wine
1 clove garlic, crushed
1 teaspoon brown sugar
salt
freshly ground black pepper
2 teaspoons Worcestershire sauce

Mix the ingredients together as above.

# SAVOURY BUTTERS

Savoury butters add a touch of luxury to barbecue food. Make ahead and form into a roll shape, then wrap in foil. Keep in the fridge for a month, freezer compartment of the fridge for two months or the freezer for four months. Partially thaw, then cut into slices to serve on top of steaks, chops or fish.

## Devilled Butter

2 level tablespoons dry English mustard
2 tablespoons Worcestershire sauce
4 oz (100 g) softened butter

Cream together the mustard and Worcestershire sauce and work into the softened butter. Leave in the refrigerator until it starts to become firm, then shape into a roll and wrap in foil. Chill until hard, then serve cut in slices on barbecued pork chops or gammon steaks.

Keep in the refrigerator for up to one month.

## Horseradish Butter

4 oz (100 g) softened butter
1 level tablespoon horseradish sauce
1 teaspoon Worcestershire sauce

Cream the butter with the horseradish and Worcestershire sauce. Leave in the refrigerator and then shape and chill as for Devilled Butter.

Serve with steaks, beefburgers, trout or mackerel.

## Curry Butter

1 level teaspoon curry powder
1 level teaspoon Worcestershire sauce
1 teaspoon lemon juice
1 tablespoon chopped mango chutney
4 oz (100 g) softened butter

Blend the curry powder, Worcestershire sauce, lemon juice and mango chutney together and work into the softened butter. Leave in the refrigerator and then shape and chill as for Devilled Butter.

    Serve with lamb chops, chicken joints or steaks.

## Maître d'Hôtel Butter

4 oz (100 g) softened butter
juice of ½ a lemon
1 tablespoon finely chopped parsley
ground black pepper

Cream all the ingredients together, then leave in the refrigerator and shape and chill as for Devilled Butter.

    Serve with fish or steaks.

## Garlic Butter

2 cloves garlic, crushed
ground black pepper
1 teaspoon chopped mixed fresh herbs
1 teaspoon chopped parsley
4 oz (100 g) softened butter

Cream all the ingredients together, then leave in the refrigerator and shape and chill as for Devilled Butter.

    Serve on any simply cooked barbecued food or on garlic bread to accompany the food (see over).

## Garlic Bread

1 French loaf
4 oz (100 g) Garlic Butter

Heat the oven to 400°F (200°C), gas 6.

Cut the loaf into 1 in. (2.5 cm) slices to within ½ in. (1.25 cm) of the bottom. Spread the slices on each side with garlic butter and press together again, then wrap in foil.

Bake in the oven for 15 minutes, then transfer to the edge of the barbecue to keep warm until required.

Unwrap, cut in slices and serve with Barbecued Chicken Drumsticks (see page 36), Devilled Chicken Joints (page 37) or Kebabs (page 50).

# Good things to go with Barbecues

# SOUPS

For a hot, balmy summer's evening choose Gaspacho or Chilled Lettuce and Cucumber Soup and serve really cold. A hot soup makes a good beginning when the weather is uncertain.

Make ahead of time and re-heat in the kitchen or on the barbecue. Serve in mugs which will do as hand-warmers and will leave you one hand free to turn the food on the barbecue for the next course.

## Gaspacho
for four to six

2 × 14 oz (350 g) cans of tomatoes
1 small onion, peeled
1 small green pepper, seeds and pith removed
half a cucumber, peeled
3 small cloves garlic, peeled and crushed
2 slices white bread without the crusts
salt and freshly ground black pepper
3 tablespoons wine vinegar
3 tablespoons salad or olive oil
a few drops of tabasco sauce
½ pint (250 ml) water
3 teaspoons caster sugar

Chop the vegetables roughly, then place all the ingredients together in an electric blender and purée until smooth. This can be done in several batches and then mixed together in a large bowl. Chill in the refrigerator for two to three hours. Check seasoning.

Serve the soup very cold with an ice cube in each bowl, with side dishes of cubed cucumber, cubed red and green pepper mixed with chopped onion and fried croutons all served in separate dishes.

This soup can be made without an electric blender – the mixing can be done with an electric or hand whisk but you should break down the ingredients first as much as possible. Use canned or very ripe tomatoes and purée them through a sieve, chop the vegetables very finely and make the bread into crumbs. Add the remaining ingredients and mix well.

---

### Chilled Lettuce and Cucumber Soup
for six

1 oz (25 g) butter
1 large onion, chopped
1 cucumber
1½ pints (750 ml) chicken stock
1 lettuce
salt and ground black pepper
¼ pint (125 ml) single cream

Melt the butter in a saucepan and add the onion. Cover and cook gently for about 10 minutes or until the onion is soft but not browned.

Peel and dice the cucumber and add to the pan with the chicken stock. Bring to the boil and simmer for five minutes.

Wash the lettuce and shred coarsely. Add to the pan, bring back to the boil and simmer for two minutes.

Put the soup in the blender in two or three batches and purée until smooth. Turn into a bowl and season well. When quite cold put in the refrigerator and chill.

To serve, turn into a tureen and stir in the cream.

## Onion Soup
for four to six

2 oz (50 g) good dripping
1 lb (400 g) onions, finely chopped
1 oz (25 g) flour
1½ pints (750 ml) home-made stock or
2 chicken stock cubes dissolved in 1½ pints (750 ml) water
salt and pepper
gravy browning
2 oz (50 g) grated Cheddar cheese

Melt the dripping in a large saucepan. Add the onions. and fry gently, stirring occasionally, until they are beginning to brown. Stir in the flour and cook, stirring constantly, until the flour mixture is browned.

Gradually add the stock, stirring continually. Add seasoning and a little gravy browning to give a good colour. Bring to the boil and simmer covered for 40 minutes. Sprinkle with cheese when ready to serve.

A choice of salads and dips complement the barbecue meats for a really super outdoor meal.

## Cornish Crab Soup
for four to six

2 oz (50 g) butter
1 onion, finely chopped
2 oz (50 g) flour
1¼ pints (625 ml) milk
1 chicken stock cube
1 level tablespoon tomato purée
3 tablespoons sherry
¼ lb (100 g) crab meat
salt and freshly ground black pepper
¼ pint (125 ml) single cream
chopped parsley

Melt the butter in a saucepan and add the onion. Cover and cook gently for about 10 minutes or until soft but not brown. Add the flour and cook for two minutes. Stir in the milk, add the stock cube and bring to the boil, stirring until thickened.

Add the tomato purée, sherry and crab meat. Simmer gently for 10 minutes, then season to taste. When ready to serve, remove from the heat and stir in the cream, pour into a tureen and sprinkle with parsley.

## Fried Bread Kebabs

unsliced white bread
butter

Cut the bread into slices 1 in. (2.5 cm) thick, remove the crusts and then cut each slice into nine squares.

Melt the butter in a small saucepan. Place the cubes of bread on a long skewer and quickly dip into the butter, then toast over a hot barbecue until golden brown, turning frequently. Two or three cubes of bread may be threaded on one skewer to speed up the toasting.

The kebabs are delicious if dipped in melted Curry Butter (see page 71).

# SALADS AND VEGETABLES

## Tomato and Onion Salad
for six

1 lb (400 g) firm tomatoes
2 medium onions
3 tablespoons corn or salad oil
1 tablespoon white wine vinegar
salt and pepper
pinch caster sugar
pinch dry mustard
1 tablespoon chopped chives to garnish

Plunge the tomatoes into a pan of boiling water for 10 seconds, drain and rinse under cold water. Remove the skins and slice across each tomato.

Peel and slice the onions very finely and arrange with the tomato slices in neat layers in a serving dish, finishing with a layer of tomato.

Blend the oil, vinegar, seasoning, sugar and mustard together and spoon over the tomatoes and onion and season well. Leave in a cool place until required and just before serving sprinkle with chopped chives.

## French Dressing
makes about $\frac{1}{2}$ pint (250 ml) French dressing

$\frac{1}{2}$ clove garlic, crushed
$\frac{1}{2}$ teaspoon dry mustard
$\frac{1}{2}$ teaspoon salt
pinch freshly ground black pepper
1 teaspoon very finely chopped onion
1 teaspoon caster sugar
$\frac{1}{4}$ pint (125 ml) olive, corn or salad oil
4 to 6 tablespoons cider or white wine vinegar

Blend the first six ingredients together in a bowl and then gradually mix in the oil with a whisk or spoon. Stir in the vinegar, taste and adjust the seasoning if necessary.

## French Dressed Mushrooms
for four to six

¼ pint (125 ml) corn or salad oil
2 tablespoons lemon juice
salt and ground black pepper
½ teaspoon made English mustard
¼ teaspoon caster sugar
8 oz (200 g) fresh button mushrooms
1 tablespoon chopped parsley

Mix the oil, lemon juice, seasoning, mustard and sugar together. Wash and dry the mushrooms, trim the stalks and slice very finely. (It is important that the mushrooms are really fresh.) Put in a dish, pour over the dressing and toss well. Leave to stand in a cool place for at least two hours before serving, then turn into a serving dish and sprinkle with chopped parsley.

## Cucumber and Dill Salad
for four to six

1 cucumber
1 tablespoon salad oil
2 tablespoons hot water
2 tablespoons wine or cider vinegar
2 tablespoons caster sugar
½ level teaspoon salt
white pepper
chopped fresh dill or ¼ teaspoon dried dill tips

Peel and slice the cucumber and lay in the dish. Blend the oil, water, vinegar, sugar and seasoning together and pour over the cucumber.
    Sprinkle with the dill and serve with barbecued fish dishes.
    This is a simple Danish salad that goes well with fish.

# Green Salad
for six to eight

*Salad*
2 lettuce hearts
2 sticks celery
$\frac{1}{2}$ cucumber
1 green eating apple
$\frac{1}{2}$ small green pepper
$\frac{1}{4}$ lb (100 g) green grapes
*Dressing*
6 tablespoons corn or salad oil
1 tablespoon wine vinegar
2 tablespoons lemon juice
salt and pepper
$\frac{1}{2}$ level teaspoon dry mustard
$\frac{1}{2}$ level teaspoon caster sugar
a little freshly chopped parsley

Wash and drain the lettuce and break into small pieces. Slice the celery. Skin the cucumber, cut in half lengthways and scoop out the seeds, then cut across in slices $\frac{1}{4}$ in. ($\frac{1}{2}$ cm) thick. Peel, core and slice the apple and remove the seeds and white pith from the pepper and cut into thin strips. Remove any pips from the grapes.

Mix all the dressing ingredients together and pour over the salad in a large bowl, toss lightly to coat and then turn into a wooden salad bowl or dish.

**Salad Niçoise**
for six

3 tomatoes
½ cucumber
8 oz (200 g) French beans, cooked
1 small green pepper
1 small onion
1 clove garlic
1 cos lettuce
¼ pint (125 ml) French dressing, see below
2 oz (50 g) can anchovy fillets, drained
2 oz (50 g) black olives, sliced
2 hardboiled eggs
2 tablespoons chopped parsley

Quarter the tomatoes, slice the cucumber and cut the French beans into 1½ in. (3.5 cm) lengths. Cut the green pepper into quarters, remove the seeds and any white pith and slice thinly. Peel and very finely chop or slice the onion and crush the garlic. Wash the lettuce, tear into strips and arrange in the bottom of a salad bowl or serving dish.

Add the garlic to the French dressing and then add the prepared vegetables, anchovies and olives. Toss lightly and place in the salad bowl, quarter the eggs and arrange on top or around the edge of the salad and sprinkle with parsley.

## Yogurt, Mint and Cucumber Salad
for eight

1 cucumber
salt
1 pint (500 ml) plain yogurt
4 rounded teaspoons fresh chopped mint
black pepper

Cut the cucumber into small dice leaving the skin on. Put on a plate and sprinkle with a little salt, cover with another plate and leave to stand for 20 minutes, then drain off any water.

Turn the yogurt into a bowl and stir in the cucumber, mint and black pepper to taste. Cover the bowl and chill thoroughly before serving.

Taste and check seasoning and serve with kebabs and grilled meats, it is especially good with steaks and chops.

## Piquant Cheese and Carrots

8 oz (200 g) cottage cheese
8 oz (200 g) young carrots
1 rounded tablespoon chopped chives
2 teaspoons Worcestershire sauce
salt and pepper

Place the cottage cheese in a bowl, top and tail the carrots and coarsely grate into the cheese. Add the chives and Worcestershire sauce with plenty of seasoning and stir well. Turn into a serving dish, cover with a piece of foil and leave in the refrigerator for the flavours to blend for about an hour.

This is delicious served as a topping for jacket potatoes or beefburgers. It would make an excellent main meal if by any chance there should be vegetarians at the barbecue.

**Potato Burgers**
makes four potato burgers

1 lb (400 g) large potatoes
$\frac{1}{4}$ level teaspoon salt

Boil the potatoes in salted water for 10–15 minutes or until the point of a knife can be inserted in the potato and feel no resistance. Drain the potatoes and when cooler, peel. Leave the potatoes to become completely cold and then grate coarsely, stir in the salt.

Pre-heat the barbecue.

Divide the potato mixture into four equal portions and with lightly floured hands shape into burgers 3–4 in. (7.5–10 cm) in diameter. Place on an oiled burger mesh and grill over a moderate grill for about 15 minutes, turning once.

For a change, add a large grated onion to the potato mixture. Fry lightly just in butter until tender.

## Barbecued Baked Beans
for four to six

1 oz (25 g) butter
1 tablespoon salad oil
1 large onion, chopped
15 oz (375 g) can baked beans in tomato sauce
2 oz (50 g) dark soft brown sugar (or more)
2 tablespoons Worcestershire sauce
a little black pepper
1 level teaspoon French mustard
3 tablespoons tomato ketchup

Heat the butter and oil in a suacepan and add the onion and fry gently for five to eight minutes until tender. Add the remaining ingredients to the pan and heat through. Simmer gently for five minutes to allow the sugar to dissolve and the flavours to blend.

Put the saucepan on the edge of the barbecue and stir occasionally. This recipe may all be done in an old saucepan over the barbecue, then put on one side and served with beefburgers, sausages and frankfurters.

This is a far cry from ordinary baked beans and a must in our family for almost every barbecue when we're catering for all ages.

*Variations*

To the basic recipe add any one of the following:

3 rashers streaky bacon chopped and fried with the onion;
½ green pepper, seeded and chopped and stirred in with the beans;
3 sticks celery, chopped and cooked with the butter and oil and onions for about 10 minutes with the lid on the saucepan.

Barbecued Baked Beans – a 'must' for any family barbecue party.

## Pilaff
for six to eight

1½ oz (37 g) butter
1 large onion, chopped
8 oz (200 g) refined long-grain rice
2 chicken stock cubes
salt and freshly ground black pepper
1¼ pints (625 ml) water
1 fresh red pepper
2 tablespoons Worcestershire sauce
2 oz (50 g) raisins
2 oz (50 g) cashew nuts

Melt 1 oz (25 g) butter in a saucepan, add the onion and fry for five minutes or until soft. Stir in the rice and cook for two minutes or until all the butter is absorbed. Add the stock cubes, seasoning and water and bring to the boil, stirring.

Remove the seeds and white pith from the red pepper and cut into strips, stir into the rice with the Worcestershire sauce. Cover the pan and cook gently for 20–25 minutes until the rice is tender and all the stock absorbed.

Lightly stir in the remaining butter, raisins and cashew nuts. Serve with simply prepared barbecue food.

**Indian Rice**
for six to eight

8 oz (200 g) refined long-grain rice
2 oz (50 g) butter
2 onions, finely sliced
½ level teaspoon turmeric
2 tablespoons Worcestershire sauce
salt and pepper

Cook the rice in plenty of boiling salted water until tender, *i.e.* about 12 minutes or as instructed on the packet. Rinse well with warm water and drain thoroughly.

Melt the butter in a pan, add the onion and cook slowly until golden brown, about eight to ten minutes. Stir in the turmeric and cook for two minutes. Lightly stir in the Worcestershire sauce and rice with a fork and toss over the heat until hot through. Taste and check seasoning.

Serve with Kebabs (see pages 50–55) and Barbecued Chicken Drumsticks (see page 36).

**Corn on the Cob**

Choose young corn (if using fresh it should be a milky, yellow colour; if bright buttercup yellow or darker this means that the corn is past its best and more often than not over ripe and tough to eat). If using frozen corn thaw completely before cooking. I cut the corn into two or three pieces before barbecuing if it is for part of a main course, especially for children. They enjoy a third but get tired by the end of a whole one.

Cook the corn in a shallow foil dish in melted butter, covered and turn two or three times during cooking. If you haven't got a foil dish, cook in a double piece of foil shaped to be a parcel, folding over the top. Season the corn with salt and freshly ground black pepper. The corn will take about 15 minutes to cook, but this will vary slightly with the age and thickness of the pieces.

Jacket Potatoes make a meal in themselves, especially if topped with bacon kebabs, or you could try a savoury topping.

## Jacket Potatoes

Scrub medium to large potatoes and rub their skins with salt. Wrap completely in foil and bake in the oven at 400°F (200°C), gas 6, for about an hour. If the potatoes are very large they will need a little longer. Then transfer the potatoes to the edge of the barbecue to keep warm until required.

If you have a very large barbecue the potatoes may be prepared as above and cooked on the grill for 45–60 minutes.

When ready to serve, cut a cross in each potato and gently squeeze the sides to push the centre up. Serve with either a knob of butter or a spoonful of one of the savoury toppings. Alternatively serve with bacon rolls cooked on the barbecue with skewers, and onion rings.

# SWEETS

**Fresh Melon Sorbet**
for eight

scant ¾ pint (375 ml) water
6 oz (150 g) caster sugar
rind and juice of 2 lemons
2 egg whites, lightly whipped
half an Ogen or Galia melon or a very small one
leaves of 6 young sprigs of mint

Put the water and sugar in a saucepan and stir over a low heat until the sugar has dissolved. Add the thinly pared rind of the lemons (use a vegetable peeler and pare off only the fine outer yellow zest). Bring to the boil and boil rapidly for five minutes, draw off the heat and strain into a bowl and leave to cool.

Add the strained lemon juice and lightly whipped egg whites.

Remove the seeds from the melon and scoop out the fruit from the skin. Place the melon in a blender with the mint leaves and purée until smooth. Stir into the lemon mixture, pour into a rigid plastic container, cover and freeze until the mixture is mushy; this will take about three hours.

Spoon the partially frozen mixture into a large bowl and whisk until smooth and white. The whiteness comes from the air whisked into the mixture so it is a good idea to use an electric hand whisk for this if you have one.

Return the mixture to the container, cover, label and freeze. Put the melon shell in a plastic bag and freeze too. When required the sorbet may then be served in scoops in the melon shell.

## Coffee Meringue Gâteau
for eight

*Meringue*
4 oz (100 g) caster sugar
2 oz (50 g) light soft brown sugar
3 egg whites
*Coffee Filling*
¼ pint (125 ml) milk
2 oz (50 g) caster sugar
2 tablespoons coffee essence
3 egg yolks
1 level teaspoon cornflour
6 oz (150 g) unsalted butter, softened
*Topping*
¼ pint (125 ml) double cream

Heat the oven to 300°F (150°C), gas 2, and line two large baking sheets with non-stick silicone paper. (These can be marked out with 8 in. (20 cm) circles.)

*Meringue:* Sieve the two sugars together two or three times so that they are evenly blended. Put the egg whites in a large bowl and whisk with a hand rotary whisk or an electric whisk until stiff. Gradually whisk in the sugars a teaspoonful at a time. Spread the meringue in two circles on the baking sheets and bake in the oven for one hour, then turn off the heat and leave in the oven to cool.

*Coffee filling:* First make the coffee custard sauce. Put the milk, sugar and coffee essence in a basin and place over a pan of hot water. Heat gently until the sugar has dissolved. Stir a little of the hot milk on to the egg yolks that have been blended with the cornflour. Then add to the remaining coffee milk and stir until thickened. This will take about 10 minutes and the sauce will coat the back of the spoon. Remove from the heat and leave to become quite cold.

Cream the butter and beat in the coffee sauce. If by any chance the butter cream should curdle because the butter and coffee sauce are not at the same temperature, warm the bowl slightly by standing in hot water and beat well. Spread half the filling on one meringue layer then cover with the other meringue and spread over the remaining coffee filling and mark attractively with a palette knife.

Whip the cream and pipe 12 large rosettes around the edge of the meringue.

Keep in the refrigerator until required and allow to stand at room temperature for two to three hours before serving.

---

**Fresh Fruit Salad**
for eight

4 oz (100 g) granulated sugar
¼ pint (125 ml) water
juice of half a lemon and strips of lemon peel
2 oranges
8 oz (200 g) eating apples
8 oz (200 g) green grapes
1 small melon
1 small pineapple

Place the sugar, water and lemon juice and rind in a small saucepan and heat over a low heat until the sugar has dissolved. Strain into a bowl and leave to cool.

Peel the oranges and cut into segments and add to the syrup.

Peel, core and slice the apples and stir into the syrup so that they are thoroughly coated to prevent discolouring.

Remove pips from grapes and, if liked, the skin. Cut the melon into quarters, remove the seeds and cut the flesh into small cubes. Peel the pineapple, cut into slices and remove the core, then cut into cubes. Add to the syrup with the grapes and melon. Mix thoroughly, cover the bowl and leave in a cool place overnight for the fruit to marinade.

Turn into a serving dish and serve with spoonfuls of thick cream.

For a special occasion add a drained can of lychees to the fruit salad or a sliced kiwi fruit.

## Austrian Chocolate Rum Torte
for eight

*Torte*
1 rounded tablespoon cocoa
2 tablespoons hot water
4 oz (100 g) soft margarine
4 oz (100 g) caster sugar
2 large eggs
4 oz (100 g) self-raising flour
1 level teaspoon baking powder

*Icing*
1½ oz (37 g) butter
1 oz (25 g) cocoa, sieved
2 tablespoons rum
1 tablespoon milk
4 oz (100 g) icing sugar, sieved
¼ pint (125 ml) double cream, whipped

Heat the oven to 325°F (160°C), gas 3. Grease and line with a circle of greased greaseproof paper two 7 in. (17.5 cm) sandwich tins.

Blend the cocoa with the hot water in a large bowl and leave to cool. Add the soft margarine, caster sugar, eggs, flour and baking powder and beat with a wooden spoon for two to three minutes. Divide the mixture between the prepared tins and bake in the oven for 25–35 minutes until the cake has shrunk slightly from the sides of the tin and the centre of the cake springs back when lightly pressed with a finger. Turn out and leave to cool on a wire rack.

Now make the icing: melt the butter in a small saucepan, stir in the cocoa and cook over a gentle heat for one minute. Remove from the heat and add the rum, milk and icing sugar. Beat well until a spreading consistency.

Put one cake on a serving dish and spread over a thin layer of chocolate icing, cover with two-thirds of the whipped cream. Sandwich the cakes together and spread the remaining icing over the top. Leave to set and then pipe the remaining double cream around the edge of the cake.

A very special cake that freezes for up to two months. Open freeze first until frozen solid, then carefully put in a plastic container or box until needed. Thaw in the refrigerator overnight and then keep there until ready to serve.

---

### Caramelised Bananas
for four to six

8 bananas
2 oz (50 g) butter
¼ pint (125 ml) apple juice
2 oz (50 g) demerara sugar

Peel and slice the bananas. Melt the butter in a large frying pan and fry the bananas until slightly coloured. Add the apple juice and sugar and boil rapidly until thick and treacly.

Serve at once with cream.

**Raspberry Shortbread**
for eight

3½ oz (87 g) plain flour
1 oz (25 g) custard powder
1½ oz (37 g) caster sugar
3 oz (75 g) butter, slightly softened
¾ lb (300 g) raspberries
3 tablespoons redcurrant jelly
a little whipped cream to decorate

Sift the flour and custard powder into a bowl, stir in the sugar and add the butter cut in small pieces, Rub in until the mixture resembles fine breadcrumbs. Knead together, then turn on to a table and knead lightly for three minutes until the mixture is smooth. Roll or pat out the shortbread on a baking sheet to a round ¼ in. (½ cm) thick and 8 in. (20 cm) in diameter, crimp the edges and leave to chill in the refrigerator for 20 minutes.

Heat the oven to 325°F (160°C), gas 3, and bake the shortbread for 25–30 minutes until a pale golden brown. Leave to cool on the baking sheet.

When quite cold transfer to a serving dish. Arrange the raspberries over the top. Heat the redcurrant jelly in a small pan until dissolved and smooth, brush over the raspberries and leave to set.

When quite cold decorate with whipped cream.

# DRINKS

## Cider and Orange Cooler
serves 16 glasses

1 bottle dry cider
1 bottle dry white wine
thinly cut orange rind
1 wine glass sherry
1 wine glass brandy
thin slices of orange

Chill the dry cider and wine.

Place the orange peel in a large jug or bowl with the sherry and leave to stand for 30 minutes before use.

Add the cider, wine and brandy and stir lightly to mix, then add the slices of orange.

## Fresh Lemon and Lime
makes about six glasses

2 large lemons
2 limes
4 oz (100 g) caster sugar
1¾ pints (875 ml) boiling water
12 ice cubes

Peel the lemons and limes as thinly as possible using a potato peeler and paring off only the fine outer yellow zest. Squeeze the juice from the lemons and limes.

Put the peel in a large bowl or jug with the sugar and pour over the boiling water, cover and leave to stand overnight. Next day add the juice from the lemons and limes and the ice cubes.